Have Ruin, Will Travel

poems by

Kara Dorris

Finishing Line Press
Georgetown, Kentucky

Have Ruin, Will Travel

ACKNOWLEDGMENTS

Publisher: Leah Maines
Editor: Christen Kincaid
Cover Art: Matthew Mogle
Author Photo: Charles Head
Cover Design: Matthew Mogle

Printed in the USA on acid-free paper.
Order online: www.finishinglinepress.com
also available on amazon.com

Author inquiries and mail orders:
Finishing Line Press
P. O. Box 1626
Georgetown, Kentucky 40324
U. S. A.

Table of Contents

[...] his hearer's mind would never be satisfied, nor would he avoid the fire until he put his hand in it that he might learn by experiment what argument taught.

~ Roger Bacon

You looked for a flower
and found a fruit.
You looked for a well
and found a sea.
You looked for a woman
and found a soul—
you are disappointed.

~ Edith Södergran

I

[for & against] LIVING AS BLOWTORCHES

You say *the painting looks like a pink Valentine's heart*
left to the rain, know flooded hearts

in our hands make the best accelerants—
what chance does the canvas have? Oil paint, like us, acts

as its own gasoline, tempts flames
into waves; edges sear,

ripple like fingertips soaked too long in a bowl of water.
My friend, the painting reminds me of Rilke's bowl of roses,

filled up with ultimate instances of being & bowing down,
that we can't help but surround ourselves

with contradictions of isolation & intimacy.
When asked how to escape a summer day's heat,

the Buddha replied, *why not leap into a blazing furnace,*
as in *extreme escape*, as in *it could always be worse.*

Feel the heat, remember: it is possible to live as blowtorches:
brothers fisting oak & mothers tonguing ash

& blackberries, families soaking raw hands in Epsom,
lovers acetylene-torching shirts & sheets.

Marcus Aurelius wrote *nothing can happen to any man*
that nature has not fitted him to endure. I want to believe.

[for & against] THE RUINED BODY

In a hospital waiting room, we watch firemen
collapse a house on TV, a home built on a cliff & a fault-line.

The firemen must have felt out of their skins, akin
to arsonists as they scouted the best locations from within

to ignite & drop the house,
to keep it from falling into neighboring homes.

Fire has no malice, it's a tool hollowing,
but the hammering boots & hearts of men bring darkness,

the caving in. The homeowner gave consent.
Not unlike my brother's; with a colon of cancer,

he must allow doctors their controlled demolition.
He understands controlled burns,

how often we set minor fires to escape infernos,
how for centuries backfires have suffocated undesired

flames, restored forests & farms.
I've only seen homes firefighters have partially salvaged

& never considered them saved,
but now I know better:

spraying water is like webbing netting bits
of memories in ash,

firemen's gloves glisten wet like blackberries,
drip ash-water like seeds seeping into foundations.

We watch the neighbors on boats watching silently,
questions beneath the water's surface:

How do we know when to leave fire to itself
or reclaim air?

Must we praise the partially saved?

ZERO HOUR

Sara says we have two choices. When traveling you can *cease to exist or become yourself stripped of distractions.* Each time I wake I lose: that last dinner with family my fortune cookie said *swim, don't wait for your boat to come in.* My mother's: *if you already own someone's heart, don't take their souls too.* It starts early; she took us to see *Star Wars: The Empire Strikes Back.* So tired, she let my six year old brother go to the bathroom by himself, then panicked as he happily watched Darth Vader reveal himself on another screen. This is the definition of depression—but before the terror my mother is a scene of beauty, loneliness holding my hand. *He always wandered off,* she said, *but you never did.*

I met Sara at the fairgrounds constructed overnight between the Organ Mountains. We slid through white sands that parted like snow, like the ball cages at McDonald's. Told each other everything & maybe less than nothing. She said *every experience is an argument for & against itself, & every argument breaks down, leaving us with Fibonacci's weight doubling down, doubling what came before us.* We tried to disappear into snake trails, valleys of erosion deeper than we are tall, but we are our families, that's why we leave. For weeks, years later, we refused sleep or surrender—rode the trans-Siberian train, St. Petersburg to Moscow to Ulaanbaatar to Beijing.

Sara says, *call me Paladin. Have Gun, Will Travel.* We always loved that gentlemanly fisticuff spitting tobacco & quoting Aristotle. & who are we now, but ladylike gunfighters trying to create order, to believe—*ruin is what you make of it.* But it could also read: Have Blowtorch, Have Mask, Have Hush, Have Band-Aids. Any catch phrase that says, *coming to a town near you—ready for wisdom that embargos & enflames on slow days.* It could read: Have Hands, Have Desire, Have Viewfinder. Any catch phrase that says, *Hey Boy, Hey Girl, ready for instincts that lead into other. Asunder.* Have Memory, Have White Flag. Yes, any catch phrase that says, *failure is a great lover.* Yes, that's it. Here's my card. *Have Ruin, Will Travel.*

[for & against] DESIGN

In cargo pants & sneakers, ball-caps & shades,
my brother & I stood on 900 year old lava.
Above us verdant mountains,
below cooked blacktop, in between
newborn vegetation mixed with dead.
Beyond the lava's edge, skeletal remains
of an adobe home with a plaque next to it
because of course we name our ruins.
Leaning against brittle branches,
more signs read: *Don't touch*
as if we would damage the already ruined.

It was a landscape razed—
the swollen hills & sloping cracks reminiscent
of summers at the Mud Island amusement park,
our feet inside a miniature model of the Mississippi River,
our toes severing the bridges of spider webs
trying to connect river banks.
Those summers were full of Graceland
& Memphis hospitals—from a distance, flecks
of wildflowers & pine disappear
leaving only black & light like an x-ray.

DNA coded our bones with tumors,
tumors in place before we knew to protest.
We christened each in the aftermath—
the one on his left elbow "Mr. Golf ball,"
the Titlist we can never lose.
The one on my left ankle "Ms. Baseball,"
the slugger that will never hit a home run.
We tried to control the perceived narrative of our bodies,
but DNA knew our futures: dead wings
like paper kites, flowers frothing in our mouths,
white spiders calling to us. That we embodied intention,
that our genetic mutation was purpose,
even if we could not voice it in words.

*

The volcano birthed over 600 hills & mountains
as magma catapulted bombs & cinders—
the heavier fragments falling closest,
the lighter flying farthest,
like our experiences which have their own weight—
the heaviest landing nearest our souls.
Our tumors differ: sand or lightning crystal,
the base or waist of an hourglass,
jaws, elbows, knees, ankles—our bodies stockpile
tumors on the left. Is my soul in the baseball-size tumor
on my ankle? My brother's tumors morphed
into cancer; we wait for mine to turn.
Why deform our bones & not our hearts?
Why does it matter?

Encoding bones, flowing lava—
each took less than a year.
So brief & hot compared to the aftermaths.
I thought this lava, these tumors, would kill—
murder the lives that came after,
but we sprout from ash, drain water from lava—
the body adapts—neon lichen breaks lava-
rock into soil, richer than before.

That day, the lava seemed at the threshold
of disintegration as if our weight would sink us both.
Yet the ground did not cave, just flaked like skin
when singed. Cracks between veins were cauterized
like my brother's stomach scar
that canyons as it heals.

How long before the lava cooled?
I imagined I felt heat from beneath,
but my brother said it's only the sun & I must believe him
because you get to lie when you're dying.

As we left we walked past the half-shelled adobe home.
It was named *Lomaki*, beautiful house—
was it beautiful after its ruin
or before?

HOUR 1

Sara says *we can't be saved if we can't see beauty, that we can't be someone else's reason to live.* Part of me believes her. But I know to hold another's flesh is the distance between falling away & here. Being born on April 13th is unlucky, my mother feels that fate—a draft at her wrist tainting how she brushes her hair, how she creams her face. Sara says we're motherless, homeless in Russia because we crave another kind of desert. When I brush my hair, she sees my mother in the spark of electricity. *Would you be a good mother?* Sara asks. *Or would you taste smoke alarm & be relieved—fire is beautiful & warm, like human touch.*

I wrote poetry inside her, on the valves of my mother's heart. (Morse code in her pulse?) Will she forgive this absence? What I do know: Beauty brings copies of itself into being, so does despair. *A bad day*, my mother always says, cholera-like. *I know, mama, I do.* I wish us safely through this giant blue bowl of loops. But our instinct is to follow disaster—why else tour Lenin's Tomb? Constant sadness gives comfort. Would I tell my daughter? I would teach her small things (to pull wings off butterflies, to grow inside a paperweight). Tell her she could be anything, virgin & whore, even though it's a myth, like the body, more & less than it seems. That we can't be saved by less than forgiveness for being what we are. The larger things (high heels, love) hurt more when you fall from them. I would tell her after she fell—then it would be easier to show forgiveness & demolition are the same.

[for & against] **RESTLESSNESS**

Restlessness is ambition in its natural state—Carl Phillips

It's what I see staring at Vlaminck's "Untitled Landscape—"

the navy sky imitates an inky sea; white rush of tide
        against beach is like the sun infiltrating

storm clouds, seemingly endless invasions:
                sea, sky, coast, each giving
        & taking beyond its borders.

My lover & I live in the shifting middle,
        not in the stagnant house,

not in the sea which is content as a nomad,
        not in the clouds so close to heaven they can't recognize
        a swarm of birds for what it is.

We are the sinkhole beneath sand & fissures
                catching castoff, salted longing
        tossing lures in different directions.

The barn in the painting, like ours, is dried blood & rust,
        marked with the ripped desire of claws.

How many wild animals have found shelter between
        our tractor wheels & hoof picks,
                blades & whetstones?

There is no shelter in the painting, it chants
        you are a restlessness inside a stillness
                        inside a restlessness.

It is dangerous to be built only on ever-
                shifting moments of need.

I think Vlaminck infused the painting
      with all his personal cloudburst & downpour,

to give it a distinct form,   a form he could push
      away from,   from time to time.

      My friend, I'm looking
for a landscape to paint my own monsoons into.

HOUR 1

Sara says, *hush, we are not Rodin's marble not the Eternal Spring, not the prizefight between Poet & Muse*—I *hush*, always, as if *hush* makes up my brain matter, but the *hush* inside is the same as the *hush* in a plane, a muffle. Sara understands, yet doesn't acknowledge these delays from eye input to brain, the static between spoken to & speaking—*hush* as a directional degree. The *hush* of driving past oil derricks. The *hush* at the end of the line between powering off & on. The *hush* at takeoff when airflow stops, ears pop, & breaths hold. The *hush* of the submerged, of being everyone & No-One's-Rose.

[for & against] THE RUBBLE OF THE PERSONAL

The day my brother thought he killed a man
he found solace in nothing real,

not in the armory of family,
not the tightly coiled highway we've driven

our entire lives, back & forth
over the rifle-narrow bridge,

past the lake full of boats with skiers,
past the lake full of island shores in drought years.

My brother has always loved fast cars
& lonely highways, Steve McQueen's Bullitt Mustang,

cruising Saturday morning full of sleep,
eggs, & maple-sweet bacon, a day

without reservations.
He is the boy who offers his jacket in winter,

the man who forgives
our two fathers for not loving us enough.

I imagine my brother as Samuel Beckett,
not the legendary writer, although my brother is legend to me,

but as the neighbor who gave Andre the Giant
rides to school after the 12 year old realized giants,

even kids trapped in giant bodies,
were not allowed to ride the school bus.

The day my brother thought he killed someone
an 80 year old man rode his bicycle

without a helmet, without care, down that highway.
There was impact: bike, car, body—

what are the odds? Not that two men rode the same lonely
highway of the same small town,

but that they would meet at that moment,
when their only ambitions were to survive a day

without tragedy, one day to believe in healing,
not the falling away of everything like rag dolls,

like stale feed sacks left to the weather,
a feast fit not for working horses but goats & pigeons,

a feast fit for poets trying to inscribe
their lives with the pursuit of truth & beauty

who only end with the rubble of the personal,
some quick & lonely helicopter care-flight

to the closest big city.

[for & against] **LIVING AS STILL LIFE**

After surgery, he is a still life:
a vase of marigolds, neck & chin painted antiseptic orange.
He is disrobed of his handyman plumage: grit-sweat,
ripped jeans & plumber crack.

Why a still life? A surgeon split his breastbone,
rearranged lungs & blood vessels, plucked a plum
from the ceiling of his heart. Then wired his chest back together
& plumbed his skin with adhesive.

You ask, *what is a plum worth? It cannot help his heart rise & fall.*
Why a still of life flowers?
Because harvesting that plum was a small death.
Because his hands are like lavender irises,

floppy things, big & bruised. But why flowers?
Why not road-kill or clogged filters?
Pitbulls, donkeys, rifles?
Because I like flowers. Because for the moment

he is pain free, more plant than animal.
Because the surgeon compared the tumor to a plum.
Because the plum is red & swollen as if plucked
then left to rot by swallows in an 18th century still life.

The truth is I don't know.
Maybe the plum was really a lead plumb,
something like a soul
suspended above his heart measuring depth & value.

A French still life painter once said *to paint only the truth*
you must forget everything you have seen
& even the way the subjects have been treated by others.
But I think he often failed.

HOUR 2

Sara says *distortion lives within us, that only you can pass your own street three times.* Three times I had to say, no, not this turn. What no one knows: We were slouched down kissing, me & my first boyfriend. His mom was driving. Every time I peeked, it was never my street. Never a name I recognized as if the street sign was as buried as I was. You could pass your own again & again & never know. I ask Sara, *can you mourn what you've never known?* The street we lived on in St. Petersburg was under construction, a face-lift I can't trust. If it can't recognize itself how can I? Not even a church escapes plastic surgery, its onion top reaching for heaven & failing.

The train window distorts—through the slant of dirt & speed, I see lavender weeds, lizard-tongues, I brought my mother as she lived like mountains in the rearview, like nesting dolls twisting smaller versions out until none are left. Associations like these are purple allergies that imprint themselves & haunt us through blood & coughing. When we hold those stems like a bouquet, they droop over our knuckles, covering the close that holds them in place. Like that single black swan, a sunspot, that spent weeks courting & flirting a white paddleboat five times his size. He didn't leave her side. A local man, a divorced sailing instructor, said "It seems like he [the swan] has fallen in love." In town people murmur, *he'll figure it out sooner or later. But he won't, you know,* Sara says, *swans mate for life.*

[for & against] MEMORY

Once a husband planted a garden for his wife—
suspended wisteria, blackberry brambles, a bench with legs like shooting stars—
  how else to rescue her from dementia?

He knew routine & familiarity generates memory,
that a single recollection is a composite of dozens:

  linear time & property lines,
    fresh mown acres,
      magnolia petals, seat-less swing.

His wife's hand feels velvet, remembers the soft nose
of the horse they recused after it escaped its trailer & ran down the highway,
  the wrong way.

That soft nose loved sweat like butterflies.
A velvet nose inside a specimen box. The garden, a butterfly farm,
  raising cocoons by memorizing the book of the dead.

    She could invent worse memories.

He places ivory combs in her hair—familiar pressure—
applies her favorite lip balm & Chanel lotion,
  slips her into the softest cotton shirt washed in spring rain.

Is the torture remembering without forgetting
  or remembering knowing she will forget?

He chooses which experiences to recreate
but his wife's memory fashions a fence against his,
  against the scent of garden verbena that cleanses cobwebs.

He wanted to design a maze that only led to him,
    grass underfoot & bare legs, dancing swirl
  of dress mingling with ankles so what he sang, she would sing.

He watches her, a tremoring ghost, twirl & fall—
        not even scientists can recreate an exact need.

Her mind, wind through barren trees,
        the moments beyond her ability, catastrophe.
He struggles to touch her memories
        in that cold, where the dead lose their fragrance.

His disappointment, a boot print, icicles instead of wisteria.
                When memory releases her, it fails to release him.

My lover says, *you must choose a side.*
        Should the wife remember, should the husband let her forget?
But it's not a wall, it's a barbed chain-link
        fence blackberry vines fail to conquer.

Through openings, we learn wanton, unwanted things:
                memory is not a viewfinder
        sometimes we prefer reason to faithfulness
lovers stay, knowing how to punish us

HOUR 3

Sara says all roads lead inward. The trans-Siberian train only leaves Moscow at night, the station domed like an inverted pool—when I was young, I stepped into a deep end, sunk, stood under & waited. The train is a waiting room of vodka, cocaine, & fortune tellers, compartments without locks so we can pass Stoli or read palms. I keep my palms clinched. Once I told my mother *you think you should always be happy so you end up sad*. Does she believe me? Sara says it doesn't matter. That to get out of drowning you have to breathe, & that is how you drown—you open, you flood.

[for & against] **LIVING AS STORY**

I can't sleep, Sara says, *tell me a story.*

Once, a girl wanted to turn herself into a benediction machine,
arrived at the St. Petersburg airport at two after midnight.

Sara says, *you need specifics.*

It was deserted; the airport was like every other airport,
you can see the blankness of it,
beige walls decorated with men & machine guns.

Why her? Why here?

She's running away, wanted forgiveness,
to write in a country where it once meant life & death.
Brown hair, jeans, a sign on her forehead
that read "break me."

A good story must have conflict, Sara says.

The girl wanted to write, but what did she know?
Her hands were myths, never still, never concrete details,
always defining & redefining & so often wrong.
She didn't speak Russian. She walked into the night.

Sara says, *you need action.*

There were no official taxicabs, no other
women at two a.m.

But it isn't enough, Sara says, *you need to open her up,
watch her realize empathy is difficult to learn.*

Here it is: the woman shot a man in Reno,
thought sex equaled love, that love was married
to forgiveness, that love was bruised
or not bruised, not gray like a dead man's fists.

It is time someone lost something, Sara says.

Men pushed themselves away from black cars,
walked towards the girl; they smelled American, tourist.
Only one taxi-man could win. He was mid-40s & wore
a pink shirt scarred with the word cocaine.

They danced. A ride to the hostel in exchange
for 80 dollars, no 40, no 60. He grabbed her bag.
She didn't ask his name.

When does he pull a knife? Sara asks.

The car felt like a prison. The girl remembered sitting
in county lockup with bloody hands.
Watched neon lights flash by, carved out meanings—
a liquor store, a pharmacy. He could take
her anywhere: hostel or deserted park.
She thought a hand on the door made her safe.

The story needs closure, Sara says.

Okay. Here it goes. A girl arrived alone
at the St. Petersburg airport at two a.m. She thought,
what the hell have I gotten myself into— she paid
a one-armed man to drive her to the hostel.

They passed an old cathedral, the entrance doors
as tall & notched as heaven. He pulled onto a block
under construction. Tarps, crime scene tape, piles of wood
& metal poles claimed the sidewalk. She couldn't open
the car door. It was locked. A car passed by & honked
so loudly she thought a gunshot went off. Maybe
his definition of love is better than mine, she thought.
Whatever happened next, she forgave.

II

[for & against] BLACKBERRIES
& OTHER BEAUTIFUL THINGS

Behind our house, blackberry brambles grew wild & thick.
Inside, my brother & I played hide

& seek with spider webs & frogs that sought
solace in the thickest parts, trapping

everything smaller than ourselves in mason jars,
creating blackberry homes with blackberry beds,

blackberry trampolines & chandeliers—
as if we knew the right degree

of love & I-told-you-so to make a home,
ours already built on wind-blown vines of

our mother's depression.
We scratched skin, began to feed blackberries

blood that beaded wrists & shins,
took life into our hands, war-painted

with blackberries, purple anger
smeared onto each other's faces, rage that stained us

even after sunburn peeled away layers.
Stains on t-shirts & thighs, ankles & socks, extract

of something dark that prepared us
for something darker. Blackberries swung

like spider bodies & spider eyes—
we frothed with mouthfuls of body parts.

*

Without wheels, without foundation,
our trailer house was painted light to catch light,

butter with daisy trim, forgetting bruises
& hickies turn yellow before healing.

Yellow primrose vines camouflaged our front porch,
purple wisteria choked the trellis—

my mother was always planting beautiful things.
I grew you, didn't I, she would say without seeing

her own beauty beyond the vines
we couldn't climb which provided nothing

but illusions of life. On days the vines united
& blocked the porch steps, we battled

to leave, vines snaking & clinching our hands
& faces until our outsides were as bruised

& tender as our mother's insides.
But when I crushed a dozen small buds between

my two small hands the clandestine primroses
never stained, & I learned the illusion

that the dead smell sweeter
rolled between my fingers,

that not even rolly-polly bugs locked tight
can keep sadness out.

I tried eating those buttery, vulpine tongues,
but since they did not live on my blood & guts,

I could not live on theirs.

*

Sundays my mother found me nesting beneath blackberries.
She would say, *there you are, Sleeping Beauty,*

praising my absence with blackberry popsicles,
but the preserved & iced never tasted

as fairytale-forbidden as the freshly dead I plucked myself.
I wanted to love my mother the way

she loves the pet store parakeets she releases,
the ones with clipped wings

that nest in feeders in the yard,
the kind of love that comes from the caged

loving what has been caged; they save her
enough to love us, but not herself—

she loves these birds not for what they offer
or sing, but as proof we won't always be

bound by our matter.

HOUR 5

Sara says we all have reasons for moving. I confess. Once I kissed the Blarney Stone—I was one among a line of heads waiting to be dipped, liars waiting to be born. A man held my waist & breathed my hair as we lowered to saliva-infected castle floor. I rehearsed a daughter's lie: *I love you all the time.* What kind of daughter? Leaving Blarney I paid a peddler five pounds to recite the meaning of my name in Gaelic: *friend. You're right,* I lied, walking away. I let him keep the weight. When I twist my Claddagh ring, trace my scars, I know I miss home. Subconscious minds do not lie. But at home, who am I? Our attendant, Natalia, doesn't like us unless we're drunk on cheap vodka, when our languages, ages, & freedoms are wasted. For years she has lived on the train, crossing & re-crossing Russia—we are not the same. But we both pretend to move forward & end up leaving the way we came.

On station platforms we play games of chance: each stop somewhere between 30 seconds or three hours. Natalia doesn't tell us, but the moment she disappears the world narrows. We wait for the turning wheels to match our turning stomachs, for flashing arms to raise & hush, hush us into movement again—we are nowhere, we are desire, listening & wet. One day we stop in a tiny town & find a lake house for sale. Sara says, *we could make the perfect home.* But I know, it is not me in that us equation, but her & the water. Suddenly, I need to believe in a how-to-survive guide for when the body floods.

[for & against] SLOW DAYS

On a slow day it is easy to tend words on a train,
to create my own pastoral:
(1) a swaying, cackling campfire
as if I am protecting a dozen goats from a dozen dark dangers.
(2) a forest with dripping leaves, hissing slide
& falling plop of gravity, snakes unwinding as if fruit
for the picking. & (3) a piano playing
the same two thick, lingering notes over & over.

It is easy to believe that these slow moments mean something.
Snow globe moments when lovers fall
like the flitter inside those domes,
like the bone chips we pass as snow, & are slowed
by water & antifreeze, insulation that refuses
to leave us to our realities. One lover forever caught
secretly piecing together a Christmas tree
the other does not want.

Marcus Aurelius said *many grains of incense fall on the same altar:*
one sooner, one later—it makes no difference.
I know that we fall,
that the order does not matter. On a slow day,
it is easy to believe. Easy to believe
that only nothing can return to nothing,
so the soul must go somewhere after death.

Easy to forget desire is a hazardous thing to reveal.
On a slow day, it is easy to forget we flee to find ourselves,
to escape the familiar that erodes,
only to fall into the same routines of erosion—
breathing, sleeping, *le dur désir de durer.*
It is easy to fall into the alternate lives we shepherd in.
But some days, no poetry will serve. Eventually, slow, clotted nights break
into snow or break into fire, & a goat wanders off
into the mouths of coyotes.

[for & against] LIVING AS INSTINCT

Hands, everywhere—*left* or *right, H* or *5,*
please, let me see. We teach
that hands are a part of the body,

but what about the jolt to stop a mid-air glass,
to protect someone falling on the other side
of a telephone line?

The way our hands lift to catch madness
edging off a shelf, to home a lost letter,
or turn over & match squares of Memory.

The way we bomb dandelions, hotly breathe
on snowmen pockmarking faces,
shave plants to rebloom—

we only want to witness
purpose in its natural state. We teach
that hands are solid, the way

everything looks impenetrable until it isn't:
our mothers' desert nails,
arthritis of our brothers' hands keep keeping,

our own bone-thin tendons miss the way gold cinches,
ache to strangle spreading black tumors.
Muscle memory won't accept

what our conscious knows: the uselessness
of action. So we shake dandelions & rip hemlines,
expect to mend the things we break,

turn disappointed
& maternal.

HOUR 8

Sara says still equals safe. On the platform of Vladivostok, an old woman selling potatoes pats my arm, the arm with the T-shaped scar, the virgin arm, the one I long to give away. She keeps the change, reads *easy mark*. She doesn't feel guilty knowing me better than I know myself—she knows the girl sweating through a tank top & jeans awed by Siberia & vodka, fears all she doesn't know & how it will not change her. *Don't follow in my footsteps. Be sweet,* my grandmother once said, *be the good girl.* But the girl on this train shares spit & hits. I don't know—maybe staying still equals staying safe. But even though the train rarely brakes, my feet push & stride against the ceiling, the window, the unknown landscape.

[for & against] LONGING

Longing was invented in a drought town,
        where grass kindles but can't catch fire,

      can't light like candle wicks or sparklers,
in the dreams of ovens & mothers

who taught us to stitch life
      into the body *like a rare organ,*

      in the cool blue abandon filling their hands,
the blue of Picasso's *Mother & Child.*

My lover & I uncovered an egg one summer,
      nestled in our ruined electrical box,

        in brambles mimicking talons—
there was a rebellious logic in choosing

      a box abandoned by us.
The door was dislodged,   rocking open & close

praising itself as an offertorium
      like a painting or a poem, betting against

      the fortunes & eyes of scavengers.
When we found the egg the wind gave it our scent

then the mother couldn't want it, couldn't
      see beyond its threat,

& since I couldn't trust its blue-speckled innocence,
      its instinct to veer from otherness,

the want of it filled my hands & I could not want
      it, not its wings, not its tiny beak,

      not its unlit heat.

HOUR 13

Sara says desire creates bodies of lies. The fortune teller & her husband share our carriage. Silent, he rubs lotion into her arthritic hands, concentric movements that grow larger & larger until her palms are cupped in his. She glares at us as if we plan to steal him; Sara whispers, *do you think he wants to be taken?* Didn't we want to be? We are pushing into some unknown—but what remains, the body's defense as dust rises & sinks into denim crevices, is a humid memory of a lover lifting my hips to the kitchen counter, tea stains & broken china cups, cups that keep breaking under his want.

Through cigarette & shot glass shimmer, the fortuneteller sees my parents as teenage lovers, lasting long enough to birth a daughter. Next, a fairytale before my parents were born: a tanned MP uniform & dark-skinned eyes. My mother's eyes, but her father's eyes first. I too have my father's eyes. I imagine my Native American grandfather wrapping my grandmother's red-Irish hair around his wrist, a good luck charm. They married six weeks later. Sara says, *we wait for love like that*. But what I remember I don't call love, but duty.

Somewhere in the middle—hundreds of hours—the sound of the train strips you clean like a whetstone. We scrape arm to arm as we pass in corridors & bunks. At home, we go out of our way not to touch, but here our bodies learn to lie, to not cringe against strangers' skin. I touch an orange & begin rasping it into rinds, swirls that bounce & dangle without break or end. My lover at home is like that, seemingly whole. Even as I cut away, I cut so carefully his skin never splits, never drips out his heart, that resolved pit.

[for & against] FAIRYTALES ABOUT GIRLS WHO NEVER SMILE

Vodka-drunk, the fortune teller says, *you are Russian fairytale,*
you never laugh. I bet your father promised you
to the first boy who made you smile, but none ever did.
Who isn't a fairytale?

She says, *every fairytale must have an antagonist.*
What of the father who insists a daughter belong to a man,
the fortune teller who only tells one side of things,
the dead, absent mother who should have known better,

the belief that laughter erases sadness?
The fairytale named for a princess defined by her pain—
she would be no one if they took it away.

I let myself be Bluebeard-seduced & beheaded.
The path to the chamber was marked;
I went down willingly, let my toes & tumors be cut off.
Anyone can be an antagonist.

*

The fortune teller says, *a boy exists who will give alms*
to a field mouse, a beetle, & a catfish. He is a boy to remember.

But what else can we offer? Sometimes all
we can do is hold on to ourselves—no one else,
not even this boy, will be tasked to put this girl back together.
Is that not a kind of charity?

The roads are always full of prickly things, of touching,
& then: the temptation to be a crepe myrtle,
to burst into smaller & smaller buds—
explosion by wing or sleeve.

When tempted, I remember the size of the world
& know we are not bound to place or time,
that someday the matter I am will become only what it is:

space & light.

*

The fortune teller says, *for three years on new year's eve*
the boy loses a coin down a well.
On the third, all three race back up.

But what if those first two coins were accidents?
The first slipped as he leaned in for a sip.
The second bit between his teeth as he dropped the bucket
& gasped when rope burned his fingers.

The third year, he thought, *what the hell* & tossed a coin in.
Or maybe the coins never left his hands.
The mind lies; why else go on? The real tragedy so far
is the girl who never smiles.

*

The fortune teller says, *walking home, the boy will meet*
a field mouse who will ask for alms; the boy will give it a coin.
But I know the boy said yes without thinking
then regretted that yes.

The fortune teller says, *crossing the stream,*
he will meet a catfish who will ask for alms.
But the catfish swam between his feet & the boy stumbled.
Dizzy, the coin fell from his hands.

The fortune teller says, *walking through the forest,*
he will meet a beetle who will ask for alms.
What the hell, the boy thought & handed it over,
wondering what worth is a coin bigger than your heart.

My mother taught me not to trust beings with hearts
smaller than my own, but I impose

my humanity on everything to remind me
of what I don't know yet, & to be gentle with it.

That boy secretly dreamed of bread loaves & pints of milk,
backtracking, invited each to his home for dinner
to cook the field mouse & catfish,
crush the beetle for indigo ink, protective door paint.

*

The fortune teller says, *the boy will fall into the moat before
your front door. The field mouse, beetle, & catfish will pull him out.*
But why that door? A competition, of course—
what could a poor boy offer?

He schemed his own rescue: he fell, mud splashed,
then the catfish pushed air into the boy's mouth,
the field mouse pulled the boy to the moat edge, & the beetle
cleaned the boy's face with its wings.

The girl must have laughed. I laugh,
at the boy, at the fortune teller, at the small victims
of the train wheels that carry our perpetrating feet.

Does the insignificant risk itself
for the significant without compensation?
Without risk everything becomes insignificant.

*

The fortune teller says, *when you laugh, his laborer hands
will transform. The past will be forgotten.*
Moons disappear into suns, gloves erode thin,
crepe myrtles explode for touch—schemes are plotted,

plays are staged, hands are bonded & given away—
at some point the story must end:

lace handkerchief goodbye
or white flag hello as mud is wiped away.

They don't tell you if girls in fairytales agree to terms,
or about the ones who sneak away, saddle a horse to keep
their pain without the fracture of laughter.

Do they live happily ever after? I ask the fortune teller,
but I really want to know what happy is. She doesn't answer.

[for & against] MY MOTHER'S HANDS

My mother says the painting looks like a hand
when you make a fist
& draw a face on the side of it,

the palm a gaping throat, wider
where the grip is weaker.
She peels her fingers away like a rind.

My mother's hands used to be dispensers
of leftover dog food, her sundeck
a skeletal ark for scavengers.

She would say we lived in a flood plain,
& although our house was a sheet anchor,
someday, dressed in thunder,

the heavens would open,
& we would embark onto the face of water.
But how was survival translated

to the animals of the ark?
Can you peel an animal's nature away from itself
like skin from a mandarin?

My mother says the painting looks like
the torn & splitting cuticles of a nail biter,
but I see a mustang dragging a naked body,

flesh skinned so fast it blends
with dirt & wild grass, horizon & shadow.
Once a feral cat led

her fog-gray kittens up our steps,
nested in a pink flowerpot.
Our dogs killed them all, mouthed & muzzled

those soft bodies. For days after ravens circled the field,
dug up the graves. We learned to kill
before we fell in love,

& to stay in love
with those who would kill for us.

HOUR 21

Sara says we carry all we need & for now she includes me & Mongolian memorials, brush piles streaked with blue ribbons of grief. We all have ways of paying tribute. Some leave no trace, live in yurts, migrating fall & spring. Some hear the ghosts of the dead, like the lost underground town in Edinburgh sealed in during the plague. Whole cities of bone tumors exist beneath my flesh. *Somethings can't be changed*, Sara says. *At least if you're ever murdered, you'll be easy to identify.* When my skin is protein in the guts of maggots my tumors will persist—our imperfections survive worse betrayals than amputation or death. Once I sewed my mother a shroud, but my grandmother cut the stitches, said *boats can't hold with bent nails.* But as a girl who's always walked with a limp, I know the bent is enough as long as you have hands to cup.

[for & against] RENUNCIATION

I will not remember that red streaks of sunlight
mimic the bloody streaks my brother secretes
or the red spots with golden auras
like lesions of his stomach lining.
I will not remember fog, an intangible cataract,
is like memory, that I always discover new ways to lose.

I'm afraid, does the world love you in proportion to you loving it?

I will not make-believe I see silhouettes or solace
as I plunge into the clouds of blinding dawn & flash fog,
I know it's not heaven; it is only temperature
& dew becoming too intimate, earthly.

It is not the soul trying to slow the morning & say: *remember.*

I will not remember the room I carry
where my grandmother bakes sugar toast,
where drawers are full of her fineries: best dress,
two handmade quilts, three disco suits. Not that other place
of anti-depressants & musical chairs,
the woman always pacing, always asking,
"could you please move, dearie, so I can have a seat?"
Not where lace doilies are choking hazards
& mirror is suicide.

Renounce, bind them at your wrist as a sign.

I will not remember all daughters carry rooms
full of things we loved into ruin: Ring Pops & candy necklaces,
Cabbage Patch dolls & adoption certificates,
fields of big brothers drawing animal clouds,
the black lab puppy full of worms I found
behind my grandmother's house,
the one she told me to drown.

HOUR 34

Sara says blank canvases want to be filled. Armed men board the train at the Chinese border, take our passports. The train shivers & shakes like a second skin, a ritual changing: the wheels of Russia won't take you into China. *You can't change countries unless you become a blank slate,* Sara says. At home, yellow squash sits sealed for years in mason jars, gold-rimmed & pressurized. My favorite, & yet I understand to loosen, to let the lid off is to forget, to pull the band-aid wings apart. I don't want to be blank, wide-eyed & ready to be filled, do I? Filled by what? The sky or an old fashioned morphine drip? With whatever saves or whatever disguises?

[for & against] THE SOUL

Truth is I've never believed in the soul,
at least not as separate from mind & body,
some wisp of light or glimpse
of darkness. But as we try to bridge experiences
with words, I want to believe everything is translatable—

there are dozens of words for imagination,
desolation, cancer: the doctor's gloved fingers
swishing inside my brother's gut like Michelangelo
mixing vermillion for the Creation of Adam
translates into bodies subduing foreign beasts,
translates into escaping puss,
translates somehow into surviving.

Sara & I went to the circus in St. Petersburg.
Encircled by unfamiliar words & familiar tones,
I sat thinking: cruelty translates: horses & tigers flinching
from whips, voices, & families. What does not: cruelty's
acceptable degree & medium. What entertainment
do we find in chains embedded in flesh?
A Russian boy said he knew no word for optimist
in his language, but even an elephant held captive
for 50 years knows freedom when offered it.

At home I adopted a goat who scraped her face
against the barn wall to stay upright, cheek joined to neck,
her horns were figure eights fused into a deformed unicorn.
Elsewhere she may have been drowned at birth
or enslaved to a Russian circus,
only the money gained from the displayed
grotesque might have saved her. What did I offer?
Coyotes, a fence with gaps, & a field to be devoured in.
Indifference is a kind of cruelty.

When I think of the soul, I think of that field,
how the sky seemed to fill in & take up too much space,
how all fields appear to be the same, except for

the patterned wildflowers & forestry, the three dimensional space
between, the flowers of experience bouqueted
in our separate hands. The fields outside the train
in Siberia could be the fields of Texas—

each Indian paint brush & barbed fence,
coves of speckled mares & hands of pears.
Hay bales & burn piles where grand-daddy long legs
web temporary shelters—are the marked with ruin easier prey?
The shade of brambles & ghost of a deformed goat,
the man too young for cancer, & the sister who loves him.

III

[for & against] WISDOM

I am failing everyone who loves me, especially the ones
with tumors. I'm failing the way cowards fail—
running away & wishing.
I'm failing the natural order
by adding sugar to blackberries & salt to tomatoes,
by not becoming my mother.
I am failing late night calls of pain
& matching blue spider veins. *You don't know*, my mother says,
but I do—we do it to ourselves, can't unlace
like petals, so we close in, steal water
from stem until dying weaves into living—all lace.
& what is the body but a swimming pool
for the drowned & drowning neural vines of memory?
I am failing implicit & explicit memory.
I'm failing metaphor.
I'm failing my grandmother & her wish that I stay
"just the same," a "good girl."
I am failing the sky
& everything that falls from it.
I am failing wisteria & belladonna, rattlers
& garden snakes. I am failing girl & woman, student & teacher.
I will fail erasure since there are some places,
some people we will never be anonymous to.
I will fail like the words "Kara was here" smeared
on dirty windshields, like a car in a car wash fails its past.
I will fail my shadow & stillness. & when I move on
I will fail movement. I will fail to know when *enough is enough*.
I will fail this ending, this white flag, this tilled earth,
& the next.

HOUR 55

Sara says we fail the promises we never make. The White Cloud Temple is halcyon, the monks vow silence, to live on the inside, but we cannot hush—home is in our mouths. We throw coins at a bronze gong 10 feet tall. It refracts sound like a body half its size, a dinner bell. For an instant, I am afraid we are only half of what we think we are. Inside the gong's meridian is a hole the size of a fist & if we cast a coin through it, legend says we can master luck. But our hands are wounds & our wrists wild, too eager & not eager enough, swooping & lifting, cupping resistance—

Sara says knowing when to quit is the difference between living & only wanting to. Two 100 pound girls share a rickshaw—so heavy, we watch the driver's calf muscles rebel; our own feet long to join his on the pedals, our palms ache to add our weight, to push his knees down, to pull all the muscles away from all our bones, to push out all the mercy our bodies know, but what power can the fleeting own? Later at the gardens we gather, roses crowd each other, wait to return the cement pavilion to its natural order. Lovers, mothers, sons & daughters walk down funnel stairs to the blankness, to the eye, hands in hands. Just before noon, a soft, techno-pop beat begins—water shoots from the center, waterfalling our heads & chins, our bodies' cliffs. A woman takes my hand, we form a bridge. Everyone dances in & out of the water, the beats, the shadows of the bordering others, whatever the story of our skin, whatever the language in our mouths & bones.

[for & against] LINEAGE

I've been thinking of the *lie* in lineage
when I should be thinking of the *line* or at least the *age*—

in a couples' photograph, when the photo
is nothing but a space to save hunger,

you can't trust the one who stares openly at the camera
or the girl paragraphed in an oversized sweater

gazing awed at the boy in a tuxedo
as he fails to invite her to the winter formal.

In my grandparents' wedding photograph
you can't trust the best man or maid of honor—

a shadowgraph, they smile as she clasps her hands together
& his arms lay quiet like ropes at his sides,

her hands, his arms all telegraphing a future of lies.
A few years after the picture is taken,

they will marry, another soldier groom off to war.
Years later he will kill her.

My grandmother will love this story
like you love dark things,

in secret, as Neruda wrote, between shadow & soul.
She believed you must suffer for sovereign love,

but I thought lovers suffer regardless. We try
to disown this flawed inheritance,

ashamed to be pillars framing a shadowed, emptied center,
to be brokenness diagraming itself—

but those faces haunt like a song sung too soft,

except the refrain

which draws a melodious symmetry of knives
& destitute bodies.

HOUR 89

Sara says *stay in the moment, expect & overcome resistance. Everything you have never known is dead to you, leave it.* This is the moment you are not supposed to look back—but I do. I want to know what I have carved my name into, what has carved its name into my flesh. Sara says, *nothing motivates more than a potential loss if action is not taken,* so she puts distance between us—we only have days in Beijing, then separate planes. At dinner, thirteen waiters line the wall, two of us dining, fancy mirrors multiplying. But we don't need help—we have already left versions of ourselves across Europe. Sara says, *I leave every time you put words in my mouth.* Her dozen hands twirl a dozen spoons.

[for & against] LIVING AS SACRIFICE

We can say I barely survived a car crash,
that I could have been crushed or blown to nothing.

I can say the scraping & bowing metal tolled
like a thousand pecans cracking,
& can only be measured by how small I shrieked,
how lady-like I crawled out, in a dress.

We can say to celebrate we will watch *Die Hard*
because we understand sacrifice,
& because the sweaters we bought have nine millimeters
stitched on the backs.

We can say, let's throw a party, decorate with mini uzis
& derringers, dangle Twinkies & ammo,
garland electrical tape.
We can say everything will be okay.

But we can't say everything,
the words we can't say are given bodies
to infiltrate our bodies,
nurse like phantom limbs of fallen veterans.

I can't say when my brother walks I see the hobbling goat
taken by coyotes; I smell road-kill, rabbits & pets
that bowed & swayed into headlights; I hear

the next victim scratching at the back door
amid the suicide run of moths.

HOUR 144

Sara says pain makes us exist. The tram takes us closer to the Great Wall—a stone zipper across once virgin lands, hips that can't always hold our longing. Construction unleashes us & makes us feel small. A cable wire lifts us into the air; we press ourselves to the window to prove the nothing around us is nothing to fear. We saw Cinderella at the Bolshoi in Moscow. The narrator watched from a pockmarked, golden moon. His first step onto this earth—never center stage—what was it? Not love or awe, but loss that he could not stand above & see it all.

We climb even though my body wants to surrender, & then we pose, sweaty & so delicate with stones braiding behind us. What I will remember most: pain makes us exist. We have cracked the lens, let the moment's light in—my mother used to read *The Princess & the Pea*. It was not the prince she wanted, but that wide-eyed insomnia & discontent— we keep climbing & then the stairs are not stairs but crumbling cliffs for our shoelaces & want. At that point, a sign. It could say *Warning, Bless Your Ascent,* or *This Way For A God's Eye View.* When we finally turn back, abandon the watchtower, we leave ourselves blind to what moves us & to what does not.

[for & against] OMENS

Rotting horse overcast by flies, falling albatross, stormy sky—
how can we believe in omens if once
1 in 10 million buffalos were born white,
& now we've bred five generations?

You forgot to be buffaloed is to be mystified

The Lakota believe the daughter of Sun & Moon
created the white buffalo, that Sky couldn't resist her,
a scout embraced her, died, engulfed by storm.

You forgot storms are a release of excess desire

During thunder, Lightning Medicine Cloud was born,
found dead a year later mutilated & skinned
by those who wanted to ingest sacredness.

You forgot truth-seeing in albino fleece stripped of sin

His mother died the day after. Doctors said, blackleg,
the quarter evil ill that strikes youth & summer, strikes muscles
with black lesions. So why the mother in winter?

You forgot to look for the future in buffalo liver

The ranchers burned wildflowers & sage, gloves & flannel,
tractor tires & chains, but a year later the father was killed by lightning.

We forgot omens appear in series

[for & against] EFFACEMENT

Stillness reminds you to flee, & reminds you of the loneliness
of fleeing. Between train stations & all-night diners
rest the best motels. At night,
almost beyond our jeep headlights,
the Santa Rosa Fever Motel's southwestern décor
seemed wistful: lizards stenciled in the second between steps,
filigree carved benches imprinting the skin if you linger,
the mirroring lace of spiders, those permanent residents,
& other small gods, stalled mid-song,
pipers of dark desert music.

This motel knows its customers' demands,
knows being the first motel off the first exit
of a town called Truth or Consequences feels like fate.
& who can resist? Fate is easier to see the farther
from home we get. Or maybe just easier to accept.

Between this small desert town & the two handguns we carried,
my lover joked I'm fated to write cowboy poetry,
poems about a rider astride a painted mare,
horizon-staring as a camera lens pans out,
as time erodes the body but not the land,
until the cowboy is just a speck of dust
& the regret he lived only one landscape of beauty.

& as my lover laughed at me, country music wavered
from the Aftershocks Diner. The night was clotted, refusing downpour,
but spitting soft reminders of the inevitable.
Even in the middle of nowhere, the night is never left to itself—
the station whites always beckon.
You would think the motel's curtains would be thicker
against the forever light, but the thin strips only dampen
light like drizzle teases the ground.

I waited for the gods to rekindle their song,
lizards to two-step,
my partner to pocket my hands & draw me from the bench I lingered on—

whoever said effacement was all or nothing was wrong—
night effaces mountains, oil derricks efface prairies,
highway are erased by mile markers reminding us of
not where we are but how far
until our next destination.

HOUR 233

Sara says sometimes you must leave behind whole continents. It's the mechanics of proximity—fingers sweeping strands from your mouth will feel more real than the memory of a girl you traveled the world with. Back home, I will drive highways too fast & alone, read Anna Karenina the same way, forget the sun there, like the sun anywhere, turns me pink with shame. We choose what to remember—the white stone horses trapped in a brick cascade, the chimeras guarding the bridge & failing, the grass courtyard of Kazan Cathedral empty except when our words & bodies filled it, the lion at the zoo who suffocated its mate, punctured her throat as easily as nuzzling her thigh in play. I will remember that lioness as a bed & cemetery much longer than the baby elephants knocking each other over, the boy finally sitting on top of the girl to stop her heart-heavy feet.

[for & against] **ARTIFICE**

Just to let you know, a brother says, "tattoo"
in Samoan means open wound,

life is a regression to the mean, the clear pocket of air
in an ice cube that heat releases

Just to let you know, a lover says, when fire ripples
so violently wood splits from itself,

experts call it "alligatoring"
Just to let you know, you say, I want to mirror that fire

Just to let you know, a mother says, car, star,
stonepit—we are all made of carbon,

we end the way we came
Just to let you know, a grandmother says, it's time

to travel to that foreign country,
to be carried by Saint Menas across the flooded river

Just to let you know, you say, "have a nice journey"
doesn't mean "may you walk in beauty"

& "may you rest in peace" really means "may your ghost
not haunt the living"

HOUR 377

Sara says fallout is always greater than what is visible. Home is a sliding glass door with a broken lock, skin I slip out of knowing a slide of a hand is an evacuation plan. But the desert is more than a place to escape from—we toured the nuclear power plant & valley of dinosaur footprints. *This is who you are,* my mother said, teaching me to pull on biohazard & bathing suits. My skin still holds the shapes—fists & cherries, clothespins & zippers—it wants to remember. Our instinct is to burrow so deep atomic fallout can't reach. The Underground Great Wall, a bomb shelter city, spans miles. Why look to the sky if you can't run? I mistrust the air at home—to think you own the space you step into is a dangerous act. But maybe it is worse to stand in a hidden city & only be its absence.

[for & against] REDEMPTION

It's just a graveyard by the sea, my friend,
not even, but a painting
of a storm-tossed graveyard
in a brightly lit Dallas museum.

It is mine though, my sea,
my window scene regardless,
a work of art divided: one-third sky & tide,
three-fourths cemetery,
wholly grieved.

In the landscapes of our despair
I can only hope it gazes at me
as I strive to gaze at it, to contemplate *all things*
as they would present themselves
from the standpoint of redemption.

But my friend, do you know
what redemption is?

We are all redeemers
in some lost, losing way,
forgotten coupons unneeded until the last
of the paper towels run out—

look at the laughter & language of families,
the young mother pointing
to Church's iceberg painting
& asking her son, *do you know what it is,*
trying to redeem his attention.

Look at how the sea waterfalls easily over
the stone wall, over the boy's answer,
how the crosses & grave markers endlessly cast off
the sea's castoff to redeem
our castoff attention.

I guess I have always wanted that seaside view,
that scene of the tide's rush in & out,
breathing reminding us to breathe
redeeming our ordinary moments.

But what does that view mean to the dead?
Perhaps infinity sounds like
that slow & fast rush of breath,

lovers swaying over granite
dressed in worn symbols of existence—
mother, father, child—

who repeat *I will love you the way the sea loves itself*
as if the promise to love as long as
the moon's sway anchors us

is enough.

FINAL HOUR

Sara says vases are meant to hold beauty. I picture myself as a vase, but we tire of being vases. In the bloody brick square, kids fly kites with streamers like liabilities. For a moment I don't see pollution, not men behind guns, but the rifles themselves & the field where I first learned to shoot. The recoil keeps you in limbo, from forgetting or understanding what you've done. The field is greener than anything has the right to be. My hands steady, stock flat against my shoulder like a loved one's cheek, like a child I carry but haven't birthed yet, the one I deny even as I cradle her & say, *hush now, squeeze the trigger gently.* The streamers wrap around trees that only exist in my mind. A little girl's fingers are in front of me now, quilted with string & wanting.

[for & against] **STILLNESS**

Even bees & hummingbirds must move very fast
to stay still, until what holds them in place
                    seemingly disappears.

You might be tempted to quote D.H. Lawrence & say
there is nothing to save, all is lost
                    but a tiny core of stillness

in the heart like the eye of a violet. Or to be truly still
means to destroy yourself.
                    What could be easier?

What do we know of stillness & nothing? Nothing—
hearts beat, electricity hums, heaters
                    & air conditioners turn on,

cars & bass vibrate roads & air & windowsills,
even the sky is rattled by planes
                    & telephone lines, the 24-7 call-in

help-me-please-my-lover-left-I'm-lonely
radio shows. What we know are consolations,
                    mad rushes to fall fast,

door prizes, complementary pens & soap—
My friend, I fear it's too late
                    to paint ourselves as still lifes,

already our wings are separating
into smaller, & then smaller still, untraceable

                    atoms of matter.

ACKNOWLEDGEMENTS

Poems in this collection have appeared in the following journals (sometimes in a different form or under a different title):

"For & Against Living as Silence" appeared in *Without Words: an anthology of silence (Kind of a Hurricane Press,* 2018)

Wordgathering   ZERO HOUR—Sara says you have two choices inflight: cease to exist
HOUR 1—Sara says we can't be saved if we can't see beauty
HOUR 3—Sara says all roads lead inward
HOUR 2—Sara says distortion lives among us
HOUR 5—Sara says we all have reason for moving

Beetroot   HOUR 13—Sara says desire creates its own body of lies
HOUR 34—Sara says blank canvases want to be filled
HOUR 44—Sara says pain makes us exist
HOUR 8— Sara says staying still equals staying safe
FINAL HOUR—Sara says vases are meant to hold beauty

Prairie Schooner "For & Against the Ruined Body"
"For & Against Effacement"
"For & Against Slow Days"
"For & Against Still Life"

Rising Phoenix   "For & Against Living as Blowtorches"

Glint   "For & Against My Mother's Hands"
"For & Against Wisdom"
"For & Against Renunciation"

Radar Poetry   "For & Against the Rubble of the Personal"

Dying Dahlia   "For & Against Artifice"

I-70 Review   "For & Against Restlessness"
"For & Against Stillness"
"For & Against Lineage"

Cream City Review	"For & Against Longing"
Minerva Rising	"For & Against Blackberries & Other Beautiful Things"
Redheaded Stepchild	"For & Against Living as Omens"
Nine Mile	"For & Against Design" and "For & Against Wisdom"

Special thanks to Corey Marks for reading endless drafts of this manuscript; to Bruce Bond and Sheila Black for endless inspiration and encouragement; and to my family for endless love and patience.

Kara Dorris earned a PhD in literature and poetry at the University of North Texas. She has published four chapbooks: *Elective Affinities (dancing girl press, 2011)*, *Night Ride Home (Finishing Line Press, 2012)*, *Sonnets from Vada's Beauty Parlor & Chainsaw Repair (dancing girl press, 2018)*, and *Untitled Film Still Museum (CW Books, 2019)*. Her poetry has appeared in *Prairie Schooner, I-70 Review, Southword, Harpur Palate, Cutbank, Hayden Ferry Review, Tinderbox, Puerto del Sol, The Tulane Review*, and *Crazyhorse*, among others literary journals, as well as the anthology *Beauty is a Verb (Cinco Puntos Press, 2011)*. Her prose has appeared in *Wordgathering, Waxwing*, and the anthology *The Right Way to be Crippled and Naked (Cinco Puntos Press, 2016)*. She founded the online poetry journal, Lingerpost and teaches writing at Illinois College. For more, please visit karadorris.com.